Edward S Clark

American Genealogical Record

Giving the genealogy and history of some American families, tracing their

ancestry to ante-revolutionary times. Vol. 2, Part 1

Edward S Clark

American Genealogical Record
*Giving the genealogy and history of some American families, tracing their ancestry
to ante-revolutionary times. Vol. 2, Part 1*

ISBN/EAN: 9783337237363

Printed in Europe, USA, Canada, Australia, Japan

Cover: Foto ©ninafisch / pixelio.de

More available books at **www.hansebooks.com**

THE

AMERICAN GENEALOGICAL

RECORD

GIVING THE GENEALOGY AND HISTORY OF AMERICAN
FAMILIES, TRACING THEIR ANCESTRY TO
ANTE-REVOLUTIONARY TIMES

VOL. II—PART I

SAN FRANCISCO, CAL.

THE AMERICAN GENEALOGICAL RECORD
PUBLISHING COMPANY

1897

PREFACE

The following, copied from the preface of Volume I of this Record, will explain itself:—

"The method of arranging and numbering the names has been adopted as the simplest for reference, and at the same time will allow additional facts to be published in succeeding volumes without interfering with the present enumeration."

The numbers will continue consecutively through each succeeding volume, every name bearing a number for future reference, as: "Jonathan Robinson (842), son of John Robinson (841); Thomas Macy (851)," etc.

This Record commends itself to all the various patriotic and hereditary societies whose members trace their ancestry to those who participated in the Revolutionary War, and other important events of our country. Every successive generation, with its biography and portraiture, becoming an additional branch of the family tree, and by the addition of new names (with references to their ancestors published in preceding parts) it will be easy for any person to trace his ancestry through all the various branches, both male and female, of the earliest settler or immigrant to this country, or even to ancestors who resided in Europe; it therefore becomes *indispensable, imperishable,* and *invaluable* to every possessor.

HOMESTEAD OF NOAH ROBINSON, NEW HAMPTON, N. H.

Erected 1790. Now owned by his grandson, Thaddeus P. Robinson.

(843)

---

(841)   **JOHN ROBINSON.**

Killed by Indians in Haverhill, Mass., in 1675.

CHILDREN.

Date of Birth.		Date of Birth.
Jonathan ....(842)		

(842)   **JONATHAN ROBINSON.**

Son of John Robinson (841). Born and lived in Stratham, N. H. Married Mercy Chase.

CHILDREN.

Date of Birth.	Date of Birth.
Chase (d. in Meredith).......	Mercy (m. Piper, of Stratham)
Jonathan.....................	Noah ... .(843) 7 May, 1757
Bradbury	David (d. in Meredith) ......
Thomas.................... .	Winthrop ....

(843)   **NOAH ROBINSON.**

Son of Jonathan Robinson (842) and Mercy Chase. Born in Stratham, N. H., 7 May, 1757. Married, first, Nancy Wiggin (844); second, Elizabeth Walker Osborne (845), in Portsmouth, N. H., May, 1805; third, Rosamond Taylor.

Noah Robinson enlisted as Private about May, 1775, in the Second New Hampshire Regiment, commanded by Colonel Enoch Poor; promoted to Corporal and Sergeant in 1775; Ensign and Second Lieutenant in 1776; First Lieutenant in 1777; Captain-Lieutenant in 1779. He was in the battle of Trenton, New Jersey, 26 December, 1776, where over nine hundred Hessians were made prisoners; in the battle of Princeton, New Jersey, 3 January, 1777; in the first battle at Saratoga, New York (no doubt intended for the first engagement at Stillwater, 15 September, 1777), where he was severely wounded and sent to the hospital. Being in the hospital several months, he sufficiently recovered so as to join his regiment. He was in the battle of Monmouth, New Jersey, 12 June, 1778, when he was so overcome by the prevailing excessive heat that his health was impaired to such a degree as to prevent labor without great pain. Upon the re-organization of the army, in 1781, he became a supernumerary, and returned home. Soon after return from the army, 1781, he married Nancy Wiggin (844), of Stratham, N. H. In 1782 he joined the privateer *Bucannier* as Commander of Marines, and made a cruise to the English Channel, which was very successful. About 1794 he moved from Stratham to Epping. In 1789–90 he settled in New Hampton and built the Homestead (see engraving) in the nineties. Died in New Hampton, N. H., 10 February, 1827.

CHILDREN.

	Date of Birth.		Date of Birth.
BY FIRST WIFE.		Thomas S. (d. 19 Oct. 1880) ..	12 Dec. 1796
Noah (d. 15 Feb. 1858)........	5 Oct. 1782	Thaddeus P. (d. 23 May, 1833)	14 May 1799
Nancy W. (d. 3 June, 1792)...	4 Oct. 1784	BY SECOND WIFE.	
Enoch P. (d. 5 Sept. 1807)....	6 Dec. 1786	Nancy E. (d. 23 Jan. 1827) ...	8 June 1806
Sally W. (m. John Swasey, d.		George W. (d. 16 Dec. 1893)..	23 Feb. 1808
11 Oct. 1852)	16 Aug. 1788	Mercy C. (m. 1st, Dr. Isaiah C.	
Marquis de L. (d. 21 Feb.1856)	31 Mar. 1790	Straw, 2d, Thos. S. Straw;	
Simon W. (d. 16 Oct. 1868)...	19 Feb. 1792	d. 10 Nov. 1856)	9 Aug. 1810
Finley W. (d. ——).........	18 Feb. 1794	John Rogers.............(846)	23 July 1814

(844)   **NANCY WIGGIN.**

Daughter of Simon Wiggin and Hannah Marble. Born in Stratham, N. H., 15 April, 1760. Married Noah Robinson (843). Died in New Hampton, N. H., 18 August, 1808.

CHILDREN—See (843).

(845)   **ELIZABETH WALKER OSBORN.**

Daughter of George Jerry Osborne and Elizabeth Walker. Born 19 December, 1771. Married, first, Joseph Brown, April, 1791; second, Noah Robinson (843), May, 1805. Died in New Hampton, N. H., 17 April, 1824.

CHILDREN—See (843).

846   JOHN ROGERS ROBINSON.   S. A. R.

(846)   JOHN ROGERS ROBINSON.
(Residence, San Francisco, Cal.)

Son of Noah Robinson (843) and Elizabeth Walker Osborne (845). Born in New Hampton, N. H., 23 July, 1814. Married, first, Abby Frothingham Green; second, Laura Ann Chandler (902), 29 October, 1864. A resident of California forty-six years. Subject to the vicissitudes of an early California life, but pretty lively for an octogenarian. Genealogist. Manager of American Genealogical Record Publishing Co.

CHILDREN.

Date of Birth.		Date of Birth.
Mary Abby (d. in infancy)....	Clara Elizabeth ....(848)	15 June 1843
Annie Mary (d. in infancy)...		

(847)   GEORGE HENRY WADLEIGH.
(Residence, Dover, N. H.)

Son of George Wadleigh and Sally Hidden Gilman. Born in Dover, N. H., 28 September, 1842. Married Clara Elizabeth Robinson (848). Captain in the United States Navy.

CHILDREN.

Date of Birth.		Date of Birth.
Elizabeth	15 Aug. 1870	Clara Frothingham	29 Dec. 1876
George Robinson.............	11 Feb. 1875	John Winthrop..............	27 Dec. 1879

(848)   CLARA ELIZABETH ROBINSON.
(Residence, West Newton, Mass.)

Daughter of J. R. Robinson (846) and Abby F. Green. Born in Boston, Mass., 15 June, 1843. Married George H. Wadleigh (847) 12 October, 1869.

CHILDREN—See (847).

(849)   WILLIAM BUNKER (GUILLAUME BONCOURT).

Huguenot. Born in Nancy, the capital of the Department of Meurthe et Moselle, on the river Meurthe, 170 miles from Paris. He fled from Nancy to England to escape religious persecution shortly after the Massacre of St. Bartholomew. Died in England.

CHILDREN.

Date of Birth.		Date of Birth.
George ....(850)		

(850)   **GEORGE BUNKER.**

Son of William Bunker (849). Married Jane Godfrey. He was drowned in Topsfield, Mass., while crossing a stream with a load of lumber. His son, William, who was with him, extricated the team and returned to his mother. Died 26 May, 1658.

CHILDREN.

	Date of Birth.		Date of Birth.
Eliza	1646	Ann	1654
William (852)	1648	Martha	1656
Mary	1652		

(851)   **THOMAS MACY.**

Born in Chilmark, England, in 1608. Married Sarah Hopcott in England; came to this country about 1635, and was one of the first settlers of the Island of Nantucket, and founder of the Macy family in the United States. See Macy genealogy, by S. J. Macy, 1868; Coffyn (Coffin) genealogy; Life of Tristram Coffyn (894), by Allen Coffin, 1881; History of Nantucket, by Obed Macy, 1835; and "Early Settlers of Nantucket," by Lydia S. Hinchman. Died in Island of Nantucket, 19 April, 1682.

CHILDREN.

	Date of Birth.		Date of Birth.
Sarah (d. 1645)	9 July 1644	Thomas	22 Sept. 1653
Sarah	1 Aug. 1646	John (899)	14 July 1655
Mary (853)	4 Dec. 1648	Francis (d. 1658).	1657
Bethiah (m. Jos. Gardner)	1650		

(852)   **WILLIAM BUNKER.**

Son of George Bunker (850) and Jane Godfrey. Born in Salisbury Mass., 4 December, 1648. Married Mary Macy (853), 11 April, 1669. The family was robbed by a French crew, landing near their house, and he was forced to pilot their vessel clear of the shoals. Died 26 June, 1712.

CHILDREN.

	Date of Birth.		Date of Birth.
George (m. Deborah Coffin)	22 Apr. 1671	Jabez (854)	7 Mar. 1678
John	23 July 1673	Thomas	8 Apr. 1680
Jonathan (m. Eliz. Coffin)	25 Feb. 1675	Benjamin	28 May 1683
Peleg (m. Susanna Coffin)	1 Dec. 1676	Mary (m. Tristram Coffin 1714)	

(853)   **MARY MACY.**

Daughter of Thomas Macy (851) and Sarah Hopcott. Born in Salisbury, Mass., 4 December, 1648. Married William Bunker (852), 11 April, 1669. Died in Nantucket, 1729.

CHILDREN—See (852).

(854)   **JABEZ BUNKER.**

Son of William Bunker (852) and Mary Macy (853). Born in Nantucket, Mass., 7 November, 1678. Married Hannah Gardner, daughter of Nathaniel Gardner (898). Died 6 May, 1750. His widow died 23 March, 1773.

CHILDREN.

	Date of Birth.	Date of Birth.
Paul } twins {	.........(855) 15 Aug. 1713	
Silas }	.... 15 Aug. 1713	

(855)   **PAUL BUNKER.**

Son of Jabez Bunker (854) and Hannah Gardner. Born in Nantucket, Mass., 15 August, 1713. Married Hannah Gardner, daughter of Samuel Gardner and Priscilla Coleman; second wife was Rachel Hussey, daughter of Silvanus Hussey, and widow of Barnabas Coleman. Died 20 August, 1795.

CHILDREN.

	Date of Birth.	Date of Birth.
Hezekiah........ ....(856)	23 Oct. 1737	

(856)   **HEZEKIAH BUNKER.**

Son of Paul Bunker (855) and Hannah Gardner. Born in Nantucket, Mass., 23 October, 1737. Married first wife, Peggy Fitzgerald (died without issue); second, Lydia Ellenwood (born 20 ———, 1811).

CHILDREN.

	Date of Birth.	Date of Birth.
William .... (858)	19 Feb. 1789	

(857)   **CAPTAIN JOHN MORRIS.**

Son of Jacob Morris and Judith Coe. Born in Nantucket, Mass., 29 May, 1761. Married Sally Coffin, 8 February, 1787.

He was a seaman on the brigantine Lucy, Stephen Clay, Commander, in 1780, and was taken a prisoner of war; kept in a prison-ship anchored in the harbor of St. John.   He taught his fellow-prisoners navigation by chalking on the floor or deck; and when released from imprisonment, was one of a band of brave and determined Americans who refused to obey an order from British officers to drink to the health of King George.   Captain Morris was, from first to last, an ardent and active patriot, and not only imperiled his life for his country, but suffered terrible hardships during the long term of imprisonment.   Later, he was Captain of a merchant ship, sailing between New York and Europe.   Naval Service, Vol. LX, p. 91, names John Morris of Nantucket as a seaman on the brigantine Lucy, Stephen Clay, Commander, on 31 May, 1780.   Died 28 October, 1848.

CHILDREN.

	Date of Birth.		Date of Birth.
Parnel C...........(859)			

(858)   **WILLIAM BUNKER.**

Son of Hezekiah Bunker (856) and Lydia Ellenwood.   Born in Nantucket, Mass., 19 February, 1789.   Married Parnel C. Morris (859), 20 June, 1811.   Died in Nantucket, 28 March, 1866.

CHILDREN.

	Date of Birth.		Date of Birth.
Roland R.... ....(860) 16 June 1822			

(859)   **PARNEL C. MORRIS.**

Daughter of John Morris (857) and Sally Coffin.   Married William Bunker (858), 20 June, 1811.   Died 28 March, 1866.

CHILDREN—See (858).

(860)   **ROLAND R. BUNKER.**
(Residence, Nantucket, Mass.)

Son of William Bunker (858) and Parnel C. Morris (859).   Born in Nantucket, Mass., 16 June, 1822.   Married first wife, Julia Ann Nye, daughter of George W. and Judith (Coffin) Nye; second wife, Emily Clark, daughter of Reuben J. Clark.

CHILDREN.

	Date of Birth.		Date of Birth.
William Mitchell........(861) 6 Nov. 1849		George W................	1857
Mary Ellenwood (d.).........			

(860) WILLIAM MITCHELL BUNKER. S. A. R.

(861)   **WILLIAM MITCHELL BUNKER.**
                (Residence, San Francisco, Cal.)

Son of Roland R. Bunker (860) and Julia A. Nye. Born in Nantucket, Mass., 6 November, 1849. Married Alice Booth, 20 September, 1877.

In 1863, Mr. Bunker, then thirteen years of age, went to San Francisco, and soon entered the service of the Bulletin, setting type, and at the same time writing letters for Eastern journals. For ten years he remained with the Bulletin, being at various times reporter, news editor, dramatic critic, and literary editor, but for most of the time he was city editor, a position he filled with signal ability. His willingness to undertake any duty assigned him, and his untiring zeal, rendered him a valuable member of the local staff, and once in pursuit of an item, he could be depended on to obtain it. Some of his best work was done in the Modoc War, when he surmounted many difficulties in getting his notes with news of the capture of Captain Jack to the Associated Press and the papers of which he was a regular correspondent, before the War Department courier got through.

A man of remarkable activity and of varied talents, he did not long remain in a subordinate position; and, in 1875, purchased the Daily Report property, and took charge of the editorial department, over which he has since presided with tact, energy, and ability.

Mr. Bunker is prominent in the Bohemian, Press, and Olympic Clubs, is active in all movements for the public good, is a contributor to the magazine literature of California, and is an interesting public speaker.

In 1890 Mr. Bunker was chairman of the Citizens' Relief Committee for Unemployed and directed the collection and disbursement of a fund of $30,000, which was used in building parks and roads in Golden Gate Park. In 1894 he was chairman of a similar committee which raised and disbursed $92,000 for the same purpose. In 1897 Mr. Bunker was chairman of a similar committee, which raised nearly $35,000 and built the famous Balboa Boulevard, and Mr. Bunker was also chairman of the Bureau of Foreign Commerce, appointed by delegates from the Chamber of Commerce, the Board of Trade, and the Manufacturers' and Producers' Association, and through his efforts, a special representative was sent to the Orient.   In addition to other public positions, he holds that of President of the State Development Committee.

(862)   **JAMES CUTLER.**

Born in Spranton, near Norwich, England, 1606. Married, first, in England, Anna —— (sister of Captain Grouts' wife), who died 30 September, 1644; second, Mary (widow of Thomas King), who died 7 December, 1654; third, Phœbe (daughter of John Page), about 1662. Emigrated to New England in 1634, and settled in Watertown, Mass. Afterward, in 1651, moved to Cambridge Farms, where he built the first house in that town. Died in Cambridge Farms, 17 May, 1694.

CHILDREN.

	Date of Birth.		Date of Birth.
James ....(863)	6 Sept. 1635	Sarah (m. Thos. Waight).....	(?) 1653
Hannah (m. John Winter, Jr.)	26 May 1638	Joanna (m. Philip Russell)....	(?) 1660
Elizabeth	28 Nov. 1640	John	19 May 1663
Mary (m. John Collar)........	29 Mar. 1644	Samuel..	18 Nov. 1664
Elizabeth(m. John Parmenter)	20 May 1646	Jemima (m. Zerubabel Snow)	(?)
Thomas	(?) 1648	Phœbe.......................	(?)

(863)   **JAMES CUTLER.**

Son of James Cutler (862) and Anna ——. Born in Watertown, Mass., 6 September, 1635. Married Lydia, widow of Samuel Wright, daughter of John Moore of Sudbury, Mass., 15 June, 1665. Died in Cambridge Farms, Mass., 31 July, 1685.

CHILDREN.

	Date of Birth.		Date of Birth.
James.	12 May 1666	John	14 Apr. 1675
Ann (m. Richard Belois, Jr.) .	20 Apr. 1669	Thomas ....(864)	15 Dec. 1677
Samuel } Twins {	2 May 1672	Elizabeth	14 Mar. 1681
Joseph } {	2 May 1672	Isaac...	(?) 1684

(864)   **THOMAS CUTLER.**

Son of James Cutler (863) and Lydia Moore. Born in Cambridge Farms, Mass., 15 December, 1677. Married, first, Sarah, daughter of Samuel Stone; second, Lydia Stone. Was one of the twenty slave-owners in Cambridge Farms, 1735. Died 25 December, 1759.

CHILDREN.

	Date of Birth.		Date of Birth.
Abigail (m. Jos. Bridge)	2 June 1703	Mary (m. Seth Johnson)	8 Nov. 1714
David ....(865)	28 Aug. 1705	Hannah	13 May 1717
Amity (m. John Page)	19 Dec. 1707	Thomas	30 Sept. 1719
Sarah (m. Israel Meek)	22 Jan. 1710	Millicent	29 July 1722

(865)   DAVID CUTLER.

Son of Thomas Cutler (864) and Sarah Stone. Born in Lexington, Mass., 28 August, 1705. Married Mary, daughter of Joseph Tidd. Was surveyor of township. Died in Lexington, Mass., 5 December, 1760.

CHILDREN.

	Date of Birth.		Date of Birth.
Abagail (m. Samuel Hodgman)	30 May 1728	Solomon	15 May 1740
David	15 July 1730	Thomas ....(866)	9 May 1742
Joseph	31 May 1733	Elizabeth (m. Benj. Moore)	4 Aug. 1744
Isaac	(?) June 1736	Amity (m. Nathan Leonard)	15 July 1748
Mary (m. John Page)	12 Apr. 1738		

(866)   THOMAS CUTLER.

Son of David Cutler (865) and Mary Tidd. Born in Lexington, Mass., 9 May, 1742. Married, first, Abagail, daughter of Nathaniel Reed; second, Elizabeth Harrington (867). Private in Captain John Parker's Company of Lexington Minutemen; in the battle of Lexington, 19 April, 1775; Private in Captain John Bridge's Company, Eighth Campaign to the Jerseys, 1776. Died in Lexington, Mass., 3 July, 1812.

CHILDREN.

	Date of Birth.		Date of Birth.
BY FIRST WIFE.		Alice (m. Nathaniel Searle)	1 June 1779
Abagail (m. Joshua Simonds)	9 Aug. 1765	Jonas	3 Mar. 1782
Thomas	18 Mar. 1769	BY SECOND WIFE.	
Isaac	2 May 1771	Amos (m. Rachel Flagg)	9 Nov. 1787
Nathaniel	18 June 1773	Betsey (m. John Bacon)	22 Oct. 1789
Mary	18 July 1775	Leonard ....(868)	21 Apr. 1791
John	10 May 1777		

(867)   ELIZABETH HARRINGTON.

Daughter of Moses Harrington and Martha ——. Born in Lexington, Mass. Married, first, Ebenezer White; second, Thomas Cutler (866) of Lexington, Mass. Was a sister of Caleb Harrington, a Private in Captain John Parker's Company of Lexington Minutemen, who was killed at the battle of Lexington, 19 April, 1775. She died in Lexington, 21 September, 1834.

CHILDREN—See (866).

(868)   **LEONARD CUTLER.**

Son of Thomas Cutler (866) and Elizabeth Harrington (867). Born in Lexington, Mass., 21 April, 1791. Married Maria Cutter (869), 21 May, 1826. Private in Captain Sullivan's Company, N. E. Guards Regiment, War of 1812, and Lieutenant in Massachusetts Volunteer Militia. Settled on the original Cutler Homestead in Lexington, about 1830. A portion of this homestead has been in the family since 1636, and is now owned by his son, A. D. Cutler (870). Died in Lexington, Mass., 2 March, 1852.

CHILDREN.

	Date of Birth.		Date of Birth.
Joanna Maria.	22 Mar. 1827	James Russell	4 Sept. 1838
Cornelia Maria (m. S. R. Durell).	20 Aug. 1829	James Russell	31 Jan. 1840
		Cyrus Morton	18 Jan. 1842
Sarah Abbie (m. J. R. Kendall)	3 July 1830	Etta Adine (m. John Rolff)	(?) 1843
Annie Bacon (m. Lewis Spaulding)	16 Aug. 1834	Frederick	4 Sept. 1844
Isabella (m. L. K. Aiken).	21 July 1836	Alfred Dennis (870)	22 Feb. 1848

(869)   **MARIA CUTTER.**
(Residence, West Cambridge, Mass., now Arlington.)

Daughter of James Cutter and Anne H. Russell. Born in West Cambridge, Mass., 12 October, 1803. Married Leonard Cutler (868), 21 May, 1826.

CHILDREN—See (868).

(870)   **ALFRED DENNIS CUTLER.**
(Residence, San Francisco, Cal.)

Son of Leonard Cutler (868) and Maria Cutter (869). Born in Lexington, Mass., 22 February, 1848. Married Emma Isadora, daughter of Nathaniel Peirce, 22 May, 1870, and Abigail Wellington, of East Lexington. Served in the Civil War. Private in Company B, Sixth Massachusetts Volunteer Infantry. In 1874–75, Private, Lieutenant, and Captain Massachusetts Volunteer Militia. From 1886 to 1895, Lieutenant, Major, Lieutenant-Colonel, and Colonel National Guard of California. A resident of San Francisco, Cal., since 1877.

CHILDREN.

	Date of Birth.		Date of Birth.
Abbie M. (m. Hubert Dyer).	10 Feb. 1871	Leonard	3 Dec. 1883
Belle Blodgett	10 Nov. 1873	Beth	16 Jan. 1887
Peirce	5 July 1876		

(871)   **SAMUEL UPHAM.**

Son of John Upham (born 1666) and Abigail Hayward (or
Howard). Born in 1691. Married Mary Grover. John, son of
Lieutenant Phineas Upham (born 1635) and Ruth Wood.

CHILDREN.

	Date of Birth.		Date of Birth.
Samuel.............. ... (872)	1722		

(872)   **SAMUEL UPHAM.**

Son of Samuel Upham (871) and Mary Grover. Born in
Malden, Conn., 1722. Married Martha ——. In 1779, he was
first on a Committee of Correspondence (Committee of Safety).

CHILDREN.

	Date of Birth.		Date of Birth.
Samuel ....(873)	1762		

(873)   **SAMUEL UPHAM.**

Son of Samuel Upham (872) and Martha ——. Born in
Leicester, Mass., 1762. Married Patty Livermore. Was a sol-
dier in the Revolutionary War under Captain Grout and Colonel
Howe. Was also Captain (*vide* Vermont Historical Magazine,
Vol. III, p. 990). See, also, Upham Genealogy, by F. K. Up-
ham, 1892. Died in West Randolph, Vt., 12 May, 1848.

CHILDREN.

	Date of Birth.		Date of Birth.
Samuel.................(874)	1793		

(874)   **SAMUEL UPHAM.**

Son of Samuel Upham (873) and Patty Livermore. Born
1793. Married Sally Hatch.

CHILDREN.

	Date of Birth.		Date of Birth.
Marion ....(875)	1823		

(875)   **MARION UPHAM.**

Daughter of Samuel Upham (874) and Sally Hatch. Born
1823. Married Eleazer E. Dodge (876).

CHILDREN—See (876).

(876)   ELEAZER E. DODGE.

Born in Montpelier, Vt., 6 September, 1822.   Married Marion
Upham (875).

CHILDREN.

Date of Birth.	Date of Birth.
Jared Samuel................ ...	Zenas Upham ....(877) 22 Nov. 1859
Naomi Sarah...................	

(877)   ZENAS UPHAM DODGE.
(Residence, 2306 Sutter Street, San Francisco, Cal.)

Son of Eleazer E. Dodge (876) and Marion Upham (875).
Born in Port Townsend, Wash., 22 November, 1859.   Married
Mary Jane Jones, 24 July, 1881.   Attorney and counselor at law,
508 California street, San Francisco.

CHILDREN.

Date of Birth.	Date of Birth.
Mabel Evaline.. .... 14 Feb. 1885	

(878)   JOSEPH KELLOGG.

Married, first, about 1649, Joannah Foote, who died in Hadley, Mass., 14 September, 1666; second, Abigail Terry, daughter
of Deacon Stephen Terry of Dorchester, 9 May, 1667.

Lieutenant Joseph Kellogg, Farmington, Conn., 1651.—Went
to Boston in 1659; thence to Hadley, Mass., in 1661.   The Second
Report of the Record Commissioners of the City of Boston
(City Documents 46-1881), page 154, which has a transcript of
154-155 of the old folios, states that the Town Officers chosen at
Town Meeting for the following year, 155-12: 1: 1659-60 (i. e.
March 12)   .   .   .   "Clerkes of the Market, Joseph Kellog,
Theo. Dewer"—(undoubtedly Lieut. Joseph K.).   He com-
manded the men of Hadley in the "Falls Fight" with the
Indians.   He joined the church in Farmington, 9 October, 1653.
Records of Boston, October and November, 1659, Book III,
page 308, contain mention of Lieut. Joseph.   See records of
Hadley, Mass.   See "The Williams Captivity," which says,
"Our ancestors say he was a brave and powerful man, and the
terror of the natives."   He died in Hadley, Mass., 1707.

ZENAS UPHAM DODGE. S. A. R.

CHILDREN.

BY FIRST WIFE.	Date of Birth.	BY SECOND WIFE.	Date of Birth.
Elizabeth		Stephen	
Joseph		Nathaniel	
Nathaniel		Abigail	
John		Elizabeth	
Martin		Prudence	
Edward		Ebenezer	
Samuel	(879) 28 Sept. 1662	Jonathan	
Joannah		Daniel	
Sarah		Joseph	
		Daniel	
		Ephraim	

(879)   DEACON SAMUEL KELLOGG.

Son of Lieutenant Joseph Kellogg (878) and Joannah Foote.
Born in Hadley, Mass., 28 September, 1662. Married Sarah
Merrill, Boston, 22 September, 1687.

Deacon Samuel Kellogg lived in Hartford, Conn., and was
reared by Col. Nathaniel Stanley. He bought land in the "South
Meadow," near Hartford, in 1691; he sold the land in 1705, and
bought in West Hartford, where he was Deacon in the Second
Church, to which he and his wife had been admitted in 1695.
He died about 1717.

CHILDREN.

	Date of Birth.		Date of Birth.
Samuel		Jacob	
Margaret		Benjamin	
Abraham		Joseph	
John		Daniel	
Isaac	(880) Jan. 1696		

(880)   CAPTAIN ISAAC KELLOGG.

Son of Samuel Kellogg (879) and Sarah Merrill. Born in
Hartford, Conn., January, 1697. Married Mary Webster in
Hartford, Conn., 26 December, 1717.

Captain Isaac Kellogg was first representative from New Hartford, Conn., and was elected to the same office twenty-three
times from 1759. Was Lieutenant Fourth Company Train Band,
October, 1736, and was commissioned Captain Train Band of
New Hartford, May, 1744. A man of venerable appearance,
and highly respected in the Legislature. Came to New Hartford, Conn., in 1745. Elected Justice of the Peace, 1745–1756.
He died in New Hartford, Conn., 3 July, 1787.

CHILDREN.

	Date of Birth.		Date of Birth.
Samuel		Ashbel	
Abraham	(881) 17 Jan. 1721	Sarah	
Mary		Margaret	
Theodocia		Norn	
Isaac		Esther	
Noah		Huldah	
Joseph		Esther	

(881)   **ABRAHAM KELLOGG.**

Son of Captain Isaac Kellogg (880) and Mary Webster. Born
in Hartford, Conn., 17 January, 1721. Married Sarah Marsh,
New Hartford, Conn., 17 June, 1747.

CHILDREN.

	Date of Birth.		Date of Birth.
Esther		Martin	
Abraham, Jr.		Frederick Webster	
Solomon		Sarah	
Moses } twins {		Truman	
Elias } twins {		Elizabeth	
Phineas	(882) 7 June 1756		

(882)   **PHINEAS KELLOGG.**

Son of Abraham Kellogg (881) and Sarah Marsh. Born in
New Hartford, Conn., 7 June, 1756. Married Olive Fraser, in
West Hartford, Conn., 22 January, 1778.

Phineas Kellogg was a member of Captain John Chester's
Company of Wethersfield Minutemen in Lexington Alarm, 19
April, 1775. He enlisted, November, 1775, in Captain Ebenezer
F. Bissell's Company of Colonel Huntington's Connecticut Regiment; served twelve months. Engaged at siege of Boston and
battle of Long Island. Discharged from hospital at Newark,
N. J., where he had been confined, sick, since the battle of Long
Island. Applied for pension in 1818, as Connecticut pensioner
living in State of New York. He is believed to have seen subse-
quent service, and to have been at West Point in 1780. Died
in Manlius or New Hartford, N. Y., 1 December, 1835.

CHILDREN.

	Date of Birth.		Date of Birth.
Leonard		Mary Ann	
Charles Fraser	(883) 22 May 1788	Nancy	
Phineas		Sophia	
Keturah		Julia	

SHELDON INGALLS KELLOGG, JR.   S. A. R.

(883)   **CHARLES FRASER KELLOGG.**

Son of Phineas Kellogg (882) and Olive Fraser   Born in New Hartford, Conn., 22 May, 1788. Married, first, Almira Kilbourne Harris, in Troy, N. Y., 1808, who was born, 19 August, 1787, and died in Cincinnati, O., 1820; second, Elizabeth Gaslay, of Cincinnati, O., 1822, who died in 1825; third, Eliza Downes, widow of William Downes, 10 February, 1827. He served in the War of 1812.   Died in Cincinnati, O., 7 January, 1865.

CHILDREN.

	Date of Birth.		Date of Birth.
BY FIRST WIFE.		Horace Edmands	
Sheldon Ingalls ....(884) 18 Dec. 1809		Leonard Winthrop	
Charles Henry .... 28 Aug. 1812		Lovell Horace	
Miner Kilbourne .... 22 Aug. 1814		Caleb Fraser................	
Almira Sophia 1816		John Phineas...............	
BY SECOND WIFE.		Sarah Eliza	
Warren Converse			

(884)   **SHELDON INGALLS KELLOGG.**

Son of Charles Fraser Kellogg (883) and Almira Kilbourne Harris.   Born in Manlius Square, N. Y., 18 December, 1809. Married Catherine Rayner Edmands, daughter of Captain Thos. Edmands, Jr. and Roxa Sprague, Boston, Mass., 13 October, 1835.   Died in East Oakland, Cal., 28 June, 1886.

CHILDREN.

Date of Birth.	Date of Birth.
Catherine Almira .... Boston, 17 Aug. 1836	Virginia ....Cincinnati, 31 Jan. 1843
Miner Edmands ..Cincinnati, 12 June 1839	Sheldon I. Jr. ....(885) 27 Sept. 1847
Elizabeth Brown..Cincinnati, 12 Apr. 1841	

(885)   **SHELDON INGALLS KELLOGG, JR.**

(Residence, Oakland, Cal.)

Son of Sheldon Ingalls Kellogg (884) and Catherine Rayner Edmands.   Born in Cincinnati, O., 27 September, 1847.   Married Abby Ann Tubbs, daughter of Hiram and Susan A. Tubbs, East Oakland, Cal., 27 September, 1876.

CHILDREN.

Date of Birth.	Date of Birth.
Ethel Lois . ... 3 July 1877	

(886)   **JOHN GRAY.**

Came from England. Had been in British Navy; had lost an arm; was a pensioner on half-pay. Lion couchant his family crest. Had six sons.

CHILDREN.

	Date of Birth.		Date of Birth.
John Gray ....(887)		And, probably, George, Isaac, Joseph, and two more, whose names are not known.	

(887)   **JOHN GRAY.**

Son of John Gray (886). Born in the eastern part of New England, probably about 1680. Married Ruth Hebbard, 28 April, 1704, in Beverly, Mass. She was born in Windham, Conn., 6 August, 1683, and was the daughter of John and Ruth Hebbard. After the death of her husband, and on 8 November, 1712, she married Benjamin Webster, in Beverly, Mass. He died 29 February, 1712.

CHILDREN.

	Date of Birth.		Date of Birth.
Ruth.........................	5 Jan. 1704	John ....(888)	17 May 1707

(888)   **JOHN GRAY.**

Son of John Gray (887) and Ruth Hebbard. Born in Beverly, Mass., 17 May, 1707. Married Anne Hebbard, at Windham, Conn., 26 February, 1728. In 1729, he united with the Congregational Church, at Windham, Conn. Between 1734 and 1736, he seems to have moved from Windham, Conn., to Lebanon, in the neighboring county of New London, where he remained for several years, and then moved to Sharon, in Litchfield County, Conn. He took up arms in defence of the frontier settlements, and his name appears as a member of Captain Williams' Company at Fort Massachusetts (Pittsfield, Berkshire County), in 1755. His wife, Anne Hebbard Gray, died in Sharon, Conn., 28 May, 1746; and 18 September, 1747, he married a widow by the name of Catherine Gardiner. He died in 1761.

CHILDREN.

	Date of Birth.		Date of Birth.
Anne........................	18 Nov. 1729	Silas	8 May, 1748
Joseph	12 June 1732	Sarah	4 Apr. 1750
Adah........	18 Mar. 1734	Darius	18 June 1752
Nathaniel	17 Mar. 1736	William	22 May 1754
John............. (889) 13 Dec. (N. S.) 1739		Daniel	4 June 1756
Ruth	4 June 1744	James........................	3 Aug. 1759
Jerusha	2 Apr. 1746		

(889)   **JOHN GRAY.**

Son of John Gray (888) and Anne Hebbard. Born in
Lebanon, Conn., 13 December, 1739. Considering himself
neglected by his stepmother, he left home; he was met on the
road by the pastor of the parish, Rev. Cotton Mather Smith,
who took him (after hearing his story) to the Selectmen, who,
with the consent of the father, bound him until of age to the
pastor. He married Betsey (Elizabeth) Skeel, 16 November,
1763, who was born at New Milford, Conn., 15 December, 1745.
He was a staunch patriot, and the public official records show he
was chosen to the responsible position of member of Committee
of Public Safety for King's District, 6 May, 1777, and served
during that year. It is said of him that when the army was in
need, he would slaughter and send to it his last bullock. When
the advance of Burgoyne's army required more volunteers at the
front, he promptly shouldered his musket and joined the ranks.
He participated in the battle of Stillwater and the triumph of
Saratoga. He took letters from the church at Sharon, and united
with the church at New Concord; but having become a Restora-
tionist, was separated from it, though still a vigorous Sabbatarian
and one of the informing officers to see to the strict enforcement
of the Sabbath laws. He died, 22 September, 1822.

CHILDREN.

	Date of Birth.		Date of Birth.
Jerusha	29 Aug. 1764	Alfred	24 Mar. 1775
Betsey	13 Apr. 1766	Annie	8 Oct. 1776
Mabel	10 Nov. 1767	Alfred	29 July 1778
John	15 Dec. 1769	Edward	20 June 1780
Edward	24 Sept. 1771	Reuben	15 Aug. 1782
Nathaniel	(890) 14 Aug. 1773	Margaret	15 Jan. 1785

(890)   **NATHANIEL GRAY.**

Son of John Gray (889) and Betsey (Elizabeth) Skeel. Born
in Canaan, Columbia Co., N. Y., 14 August, 1773. He was a
farmer, living an exemplary and useful life, and was an influential
man in church and political circles. He was an elder in the
church, and usually held some public office. He married Sarah
Butler, in Sherburne, N. Y., 5 September, 1797, who was born
in Weathersfield, Conn., 30 April, 1771, and died in Mt. Carroll,
Ill., April, 1852. He died, 10 April, 1845.

CHILDREN.

	Date of Birth.		Date of Birth.
Parnelia	4 Sept. 1798	Calvin ....(891)	1 Sept. 1805
Milan	4 Jan. 1800	Reuben H.	3 Mar. 1816
Francis	26 Mar. 1803		

(891)   CALVIN GRAY.

Son of Nathaniel Gray (890) and Sarah Butler. Born in Ger-
vian, N. Y., 1 September, 1805. He married Abigail North
Spaulding, in Franklinville, Cattaraugus Co., N.Y., 7 June, 1842,
who was born at Lisle, Broome Co., N.Y., 14 May, 1815. He
was a Presbyterian minister, and engaged almost his entire life in
the work of a home missionary. He died in Fort Dodge, Ia.,
20 March, 1885.

CHILDREN.

	Date of Birth.		Date of Birth.
Lyman Calvin.	26 Oct. 1843	Henry North	7 July 1851
Carlton Rinewalt	7 Jan. 1847	Howard Edmund	7 Oct. 1853
Linus Shepard	25 July 1849	Roscoe Spaulding .... .. (892)	7 Apr. 1857

(892)   ROSCOE SPAULDING GRAY.

(Residence, Auburn, N.Y.; Fort Dodge, Ia.; Oakland, Cal.)

Son of Calvin Gray (891) and Abigail North Spaulding. Born
in Mt. Carroll, Ill., 7 April, 1857. Married Mary Fox, at San
Francisco, Cal., 12 May, 1887, who was a daughter of Charles
N. Fox and Mary S. Fox, born in Redwood City, Cal., 7 Octo-
ber, 1866. He was for years a shorthand reporter (official in
Iowa), and for some two years with William T. Coleman in San
Francisco, Cal.; admitted to the Bar in 1890.

CHILDREN.

	Date of Birth.		Date of Birth.
Mary	24 Mar. 1888	Roscoe Nelson	24 Dec. 1892
Charles Calvin	4 June 1889	Kenneth	3 Nov. 1894
Elizabeth	13 Mar. 1891		

(893)   PETER COFFYN.

Son of Nicholas Coffyn and Joan ——. Born in England,
about 1580. Married Joan Thember (or Thumber). Died in
England, about 1627.

CHILDREN.

	Date of Birth.		Date of Birth.
Tristram ....(894)	1605	Deborah	
John		Eunice	
Joan		Mary	

ROSCOE SPAULDING GRAY. S. A. R.

Cristram Coffyn

*First Chief Magistrate of the Islands of
Nantuckett and Tuckanuckett
June 9th 1671*

COAT-OF-ARMS OF
TRISTRAM COFFYN (COFFIN).

(894)   **TRISTRAM COFFYN (COFFIN).**

Son of Peter Coffyn (893) and Joan Thember. Born in Brixton, near Plymouth, England, about 1605. Married Dionis Stevens, daughter of Robert Stevens of Brixton, about 1630, and emigrated to America about 1642. He lived successively in Salisbury, Haverhill, and Newbury, Mass.; and finally, with Thomas Macy (851) and others, purchased the Island of Nantucket. See "Life of Tristram Coffyn," by Allen Coffin, Nantucket, 1881, and Macy Genealogy. He died in Nantucket, 2 October, 1681.

CHILDREN.

	Date of Birth.		Date of Birth.
Peter ....(915)	1631	Deborah (d. 8 Dec. 1642) ..... 16 Nov. 1642
Tristram, Jr.. .... (917)	1652	Mary................. ... (918) 20 Feb. 1645
Elizabeth	1634	John ....(896) 30 Oct. 1647
James ....(895) 12 Aug. 1640		Stephen ....(919) 10 May 1652
John (d. 30 Oct. 1642)		

(895)   **JAMES COFFIN.**

Son of Tristram Coffin (894) and Dionis Stevens. Born in England, 12 August, 1640. Married Mary, daughter of John and Abigail Severance of Salisbury, Mass., 3 December, 1663. He was one of the first settlers of Nantucket; moved to Dover, N. H., where he lived in 1668; returned to Nantucket, and died there 28 July, 1720.

CHILDREN.

	Date of Birth.		Date of Birth.
Mary.......... .... 18 Apr. 1665		Joseph (m. Bethiah Macy).... 4 Feb. 1680
James, Jr..............		Elizabeth ....
Nathaniel (m. Damaris Gayer)	1671	Benjamin (d.) .... 28 Aug. 1683
John		Ruth. ....
Dinah..............		Abigail ....(901)
Deborah		Experience (d. young) ......
Ebenezer .... 30 May 1678		Jonathan.................... 28 Aug. 1692

(896)   **JOHN COFFIN.**

Son of Tristram Coffin (894) and Dionis Stevens. Born in Haverhill, Mass., 30 October, 1647. Married Deborah Austin (910). He died in Edgartown, Mass., 5 September, 1711.

CHILDREN.

	Date of Birth.		Date of Birth.
Lydia (m. 1st, John Logan; 2d, John Draper; 3d, Thos. Thaxter)	1 June 1669	Enoch (m. Beulah Eddy)....	1678
Peter (m. 1st, Christian Condy; 2d, Hope Gardner)	5 Aug. 1671	Samuel (m. Miriam Gardner) Hannah (m. Ben. Gardner) .. Tristram (m. Mary Bunker).. Deborah ....(921)	
John, Jr.	10 Feb. 1673	Elizabeth (d. single)	
Love (d. single)....	23 Apr. 1676	Benjamin	23 Aug. 1683

(897)   RICHARD GARDNER.

Son of Thomas Gardner (906) and Margaret Frier. Married Sarah Shattuck in 1652, a daughter of Samuel Shattuck and his step-mother, Damaris ——. She died in 1724, aged ninety-two years. He and wife were excommunicated from the church in Salem for attending Quaker meetings. He died 23 January, 1688.

CHILDREN.

	Date of Birth.		Date of Birth.
Sarah	(934) about 1653	Love (m. Jas. Coffin)	
Deborah	(900) 12 Feb. 1655	Hope (m. John Coffin)	
Richard, Jr. (m. Mary Austin)		Joseph (m. Bethiah Macy)	
James (m. 1st Mary Starbuck; 2d, Mary Coffin; 3d, Patience Folger)		Nathaniel	(898) Nov. 1669
		Miriam (m. John Worth)	
		Damaris	

(898)   NATHANIEL GARDNER.

Son of Richard Gardner (897) and Sarah Shattuck. Born, November, 1669. Married Abigail Coffin (901). Died in 1713.

CHILDREN.

	Date of Birth.		Date of Birth.
Hannah (m. J. Bunker 854)	6 Jan. 1686	Nathaniel	14 Dec. 1697
Ebenezer.	27 Oct. 1688	Andrew	26 Dec. 1699
Peleg	22 July 1691	Abel	6 Aug. 1702
Judith	28 Oct. 1693	Susanna	4 Aug. 1706
Margaret	28 Jan. 1696		

(899)   JOHN MACY.

Son of Thomas Macy (851) and Sarah Hopcott. Born in Salisbury, Mass., 14 July, 1655. Married Deborah Gardner (900). Died in Nantucket, 14 October, 1691.

CHILDREN.

	Date of Birth.		Date of Birth.
John	about 1675	Jabez	about 1683
Sarah (m. John Barnard).	3 Apr. 1677	Mary (m. Solomon Coleman).	about 1685
Deborah (m. Daniel Russell).	3 Mar. 1679	Thomas	(922) about 1687
Bethiah	8 Apr. 1681	Richard	22 Sept. 1689

(900)   **DEBORAH GARDNER.**

Daughter of Richard Gardner (897) and Sarah Shattuck. Born, 12 February, 1658. Married John Macy (899). Died in Nantucket, 1712.

CHILDREN—See (899).

(901)   **ABIGAIL COFFIN.**

Daughter of James Coffin (895) and Mary Severance. Married Nathaniel Gardner (898). Died in Nantucket, 15 March, 1709.

CHILDREN—See (898).

(902)   **LAURA ANN CHANDLER.**
                (Residence, San Francisco, Cal.)

Daughter of —— Chandler. Born in Duxbury, Mass., 4 October, 1818. Married, first, Frederick Hatch; second, John Rogers Robinson (846), in San Francisco, 29 October, 1864. Died in San Francisco, 26 August, 1893.

(903)   **JOSEPH AUSTIN.**

Son of —— Austin. Born about 1625 or 1630. Married Sarah Starbuck (909) in 1659.

CHILDREN.

Date of Birth.		Date of Birth.
Deborah...............(910)		

(904)   **JOHN FOLGER.**

Married Meribah Gibbs. Came to America from Norwich, England, in 1635, and settled in Martha's Vineyard.

CHILDREN.

Date of Birth.		Date of Birth.
Peter ....(905)	John	

(905)   **PETER FOLGER.**

Son of John Folger (904) and Meribah Gibbs. Born in England in 1618. Married Mary Morrill in 1644, and moved to Nantucket in 1673. Died in Nantucket in 1704.

CHILDREN.

	Date of Birth.		Date of Birth.
Eleazer	(928)	1645	Patience (m. 1st, Ebenezer
John		1659	Harker; 2d, Jas. Gardner).
Joanna (m. John Coleman)			Experience (m. John Swain).
Bethia (m. John Barnard)			Abiah (m. Josiah Franklin,
Dorcas (m. Joseph Pratt)			and was mother of Benja-
Bethshua (m. Joseph Pope)			min Franklin) .... 15 Aug. 1667

(906)   **THOMAS GARDNER.**

Came from Sherburne, County of Dorset, England, where he married Margaret Frier. Came to America and settled at Cape Ann in 1624, where he was employed by the projectors of the settlement to oversee the fishery. He was a representative at the General Court at Boston in 1625 and 1637. Married, second, Damaris ——, widow of Samuel Shattuck. Died in 1677.

CHILDREN.

	Date of Birth.		Date of Birth.
Richard	(897)		And eight others in England.
John	(907)		

(907)   **CAPTAIN JOHN GARDNER.**

Son of Thomas Gardner (906) and Margaret Frier. Born in England. Married Priscilla Grafton, daughter of Joseph Grafton of Salem, *20 February, 1654. Came from Salem to Nantucket with his brother Richard in 1666, and received a large grant of land in the northern part of the island for inaugurating new commercial enterprises. The gravestone of Captain John Gardner can still be seen near Maxey's Pond.

CHILDREN.

	Date of Birth.		Date of Birth.
John	20 Feb. 1654	Anna (m. Edw. Coffin)	30 Feb. 1667
Joseph	5 July 1655	Nathaniel	24 Sept. 1668
Priscilla	6 Nov. 1656	Mary (m. Jethro Coffin)	27 May 1670
Benjamin	3 Feb. 1658	Mehitable (m. Ambrose Dawes	
Rachel (m. John Brown and		2d)	24 Nov. 1674
James Gardner)	3 Aug. 1662	Ruth (m. James Coffin 2d)	26 Jan. 1677
Benjamin	17 May 1664		

(908)   **EDWARD STARBUCK.**

Born in Derbyshire, England, in 1604. Married Katherine Reynolds, a Welshwoman. Was an elder in the church at

---

* The date of marriage was probably earlier.

Dover, N. H., in 1643 and 1646. Came from Salisbury to Nantucket in a sailboat with Thomas Macy (851) in the fall of 1659. Died in Nantucket, 4 December, 1690.

CHILDREN.

	Date of Birth.		Date of Birth.
Nathaniel ... . (914)	1636	Abigail............... (916)	
Jethro (d. 27 May, 1663)		Esther (m. Humphrey Varney)	
Sarah ....(909)		Dorcas .... (912)	

(909)   **SARAH STARBUCK.**

Daughter of Edward Starbuck (908) and Katherine Reynolds. Married, first, William Story; second, Joseph Austin (903) in 1649; third, Humphrey Varney.

CHILDREN—See (903).

(910)   **DEBORAH AUSTIN.**

Daughter of Joseph Austin (903) and Sarah Starbuck (909). Born in Nantucket. Married John Coffin (896).

CHILDREN—See (896).

(911)   **WILLIAM GAYER.**

Married Dorcas Starbuck (912) in Nantucket.

CHILDREN.

	Date of Birth.		Date of Birth.
Damaris (m. Nathaniel Coffin)	24 Oct. 1673	William (m. Eliz. Gayer)....	3 June 1677
Dorcas ....(913)	29 Aug. 1675		

(912)   **DORCAS STARBUCK.**

Daughter of Edward Starbuck (908) and Katherine Reynolds. Married William Gayer (911). Died in 1696.

CHILDREN—See (911).

(913)   **DORCAS GAYER.**

Daughter of William Gayer (911) and Dorcas Starbuck (912). Born 29 August, 1675. Married Jethro Starbuck (920) 6 December, 1694.

CHILDREN—See (920).

(914)   **NATHANIEL STARBUCK.**

Son of Edward Starbuck (908) and Katherine Reynolds. Born in England in 1636. Married Mary Coffin (918) in 1662. Died 6 August (or 2 February), 1719.

CHILDREN.

Date of Birth.		Date of Birth.	
Mary (m. James Gardner) ...	30 Mar. 1663	Eunice (m. Geo. Gardner)....	11 Apr. 1674
Elizabeth (m. 1st, Peter Coffin;		Priscilla (m. John Coleman)..	1676
2d, Nathaniel Barnard, Jr.)	9 Sept. 1665	Hepzibah (m. T. Hathaway).	2 Apr. 1680
Nathaniel (m. Dinah Coffin) .	9 Aug. 1668	Ann (d. single)..............	
Jethro ... .(920)	14 Dec. 1671	Paul (d. single)	
Barnabus (d. single)	1673		

(915)   **PETER COFFIN.**

Son of Tristram Coffin (894) and Dionis Stevens. Born in Brixton, England, in 1631. Married Abigail Starbuck, (916). Was freeman in 1666 at Dover; Lieutenant in 1675 in King Philip's War; Representative of Legislature in 1672-3 and in 1679. In 1690 he moved to Exeter, N. H. Was Chief Justice of Supreme Court of New Hampshire about 1714. Died in Exeter, N. H., 21 March, 1715.

CHILDREN.

Date of Birth.		Date of Birth.	
Abigail (m. Daniel Davidson).	20 Oct. 1657	Edward (m. Anna Gardner)..	20 Feb. 1669
Peter, Jr. (m. Eliz. Starbuck).	20 Aug. 1660	Judith	4 Feb. 1672
Jethro (m. Mary Gardner) ...	16 Sept. 1663	Parnell (d. young)...........	
Tristram (m. Deb. Colcord)..	18 Jan. 1665	Elizabeth (m. Col. J. Gilman)	27 Jan. 1680
Robert (m. Joanna Gilman) ..	1667	Eliphalet (d. single).........	

(916)   **ABIGAIL STARBUCK.**

Daughter of Edward Starbuck (908) and Katherine Reynolds. Married Peter Coffin (915).

CHILDREN—See (915).

(917)   **TRISTRAM COFFIN, JR.**

Son of Tristram Coffin (894) and Dionis Stevens. Born in England in 1632. Married Judith (Greenleaf) Somerby, widow of Henry Somerby and daughter of Edmund and Sarah Greenleaf, in Newbury, Mass. Judith Greenleaf was born in 1625, and died in Newbury, Mass., 15 December, 1705. He died in Newbury, Mass., 4 February, 1703.

CHILDREN.

Date of Birth.		Date of Birth.
Judith (m. John Sanborn)....	4 Dec. 1653	Lydia (m. 1st, Moses Little;
Deborah (m. Joseph Knight).	10 Nov. 1655	2d, John Pike) .... 22 Apr. 1662
Mary (m. Joseph Little)	12 Nov. 1657	Enoch (d. 12 Nov. 1675) ..... 21 Jan. 1663
James (m. Florence Hooke)..	22 Apr. 1659	Stephen (m. Sarah Atkinson). 18 Aug. 1664
John (d. 13 May, 1677)	8 Sept. 1660	Peter (m. Apphia Dole) ..... 27 July 1667
		Nathaniel (m. Sarah Dole) .. 22 Mar. 1669

(918)   MARY COFFIN.

Daughter of Tristram Coffin (894) and Dionis Stevens. Born in Haverhill, Mass., 20 February, 1645. Married Nathaniel Starbuck (914) in 1662. Died in Nantucket, 13 November, 1717.

CHILDREN—See (914).

(919)   STEPHEN COFFIN.

Son of Tristram Coffin (894) and Dionis Stephens. Born in Newbury, Mass., 10 May, 1652. Married Mary Bunker (936) about 1668–9. Died in Nantucket, 14 November, 1734.

CHILDREN.

Date of Birth.		Date of Birth.
Daniel (d. single).............		Susanna (m. Peleg Bunker)...
Dionis (m. Jacob Norton)		Mehitable (m. A. Smith) .....
Peter...........	14 Nov. 1673	Anna (m. Sol. Gardner)......
Stephen, Jr. (m. Exp. Look)..	20 Feb. 1675	Hepzibah (m. Sam'l Gardner)
Judith.... ....(937)		Paul (m. Mary Allen) ....

(920)   JETHRO STARBUCK.

Son of Nathaniel Starbuck (914) and Mary Coffin (918). Born in Nantucket, 14 December, 1671. Married Dorcas Gayer (913) 6 December, 1694. Died 12 August, 1770.

CHILDREN.

Date of Birth.		Date of Birth.
William .... (925)		Sarah (m. Jabez Macy).......	1697

(921)   DEBORAH COFFIN.

Daughter of John Coffin (896) and Deborah Austin (910). Born in Nantucket. Married Thomas Macy (922) 18 June, 1708. Died in Nantucket, 23 September, 1760.

CHILDREN—See (922).

(922)   THOMAS MACY.

Son of John Macy (899) and Deborah Gardner (900).   Born
in Nantucket about 1687.   Married Deborah Coffin (921).   Died
in Nantucket, 16 March, 1759.

CHILDREN.

	Date of Birth.		Date of Birth.
Joseph ....(923)	8 Apr. 1709	Elizabeth (m. Fran. Barnard)	9 June 1722
Robert (m. Abigail Barnard).	20 Nov. 1710	Thomas (d. young)	13 Aug. 1724
Love (m. Joseph Rotch)	9 Feb. 1713	Deborah (m. Benj. Coffin)....	17 Apr. 1726
Francis (m. Judith Coffin) ...	2 June 1715	Anna (m. Richard Worth) ...	7 Apr. 1730
Nathaniel (m. Ab. Pinkham).	20 Aug. 1717	Hepzabeth (m. Thos. Davis).	22 Oct. 1734
Lydia (m. Jethro Coleman)..	23 Feb. 1720		

(923)   JOSEPH MACY.

Son of Thomas Macy (922) and Deborah Coffin (921).   Born
in Nantucket, 8 April, 1709.   Married Hannah Hobbs in 1728.
Died in Nantucket, 28 June, 1772.

CHILDREN.

	Date of Birth.		Date of Birth.
Mary (m. 1st, Paul Way; 2d,		Henry (m. 1st, Sarah Swain;	
James Anthony)	15 July 1729	2d, Elizabeth Hussey)......	4 Nov. 1737
Thomas (m. Mary Starbuck).	1 Mar. 1731	Paul (m. 1st, Bethiah Macy;	
Bethiah (m. Nath'l Swain)...	3 Apr. 1733	2d, Deborah Coggeshall)...	3 May, 1740
Joseph ....(924)	4 Oct. 1735	Enoch (m. Anna Macy)	11 May, 1743

(924)   JOSEPH MACY.

Son of Joseph Macy (923) and Hannah Hobbs.   Born in
Nantucket, 4 October, 1735.   Married Mary Starbuck (926) in
Nantucket, November, 1757.   Died in Guilford Co., N. C., 17—.

CHILDREN.

	Date of Birth.		Date of Birth.
Anna (d. 1808)...............	26 July 1758	William ....(927)	7 Feb. 1772
Hannah (d. 3 Dec. 1775)	31 July 1761	Albert (m. Nancy Wall).....	4 Feb. 1774
Elizabeth (m. Uriah Barnard)	14 Oct. 1763	Hannah (m. M. Wall)	18 Mar. 1776
Joseph	1 Sept. 1765	Phebe (m. John Lamb).......	26 Mar. 1778
Mary........................	21 Oct. 1767	Reuben (m. Lucy Petty)	29 May 1780
Rhoda (m. Job Worth)	26 Dec. 1769	Judith (m. Joseph Way)......	4 Nov. 1783

(925)   WILLIAM STARBUCK.

Son of Jethro Starbuck (920) and Dorcas Gayer (913).   Born
in Nantucket (?) in 16—.   Married Anna Folger (938).

CHILDREN.

	Date of Birth.		Date of Birth.
Mary ....(926)	1738		

(926)   **MARY STARBUCK.**

Daughter of William Starbuck (925) and Anna Folger (938).
Born in Nantucket in 1738. Married Joseph Macy (924) November, 1757. Died in Guilford Co., N. C., in 17—.

CHILDREN—See (924).

(927)   **WILLIAM MACY.**

Son of Joseph Macy (924) and Mary Starbuck (926). Born
in Nantucket, 7 February, 1772. Married Mary Barnard (929),
in Stoke Co., N. C., in 1799. Died in Union Co., Ind., 14
March, 1855.

CHILDREN.

	Date of Birth.		Date of Birth.
Obed ....(930)	14 Dec. 1801	Reuben (m. Maria Gardner)..	12 July 1812
Tristram (m. Mary Swain) ..	15 Oct. 1803	Franklin (m. Ann Wetherald)	19 Dec. 1814
Stephen (d. 1826)	4 Oct. 1805	Thomas C. (m. E. Horsman).	9 May 1818
John W. (m. Elvira Coffin) ..	18 Nov. 1807	Rhoda (m. Gideon Gardner) .	15 June 1820
Jonathan (m. Elizabeth ——).	6 June 1810	Emily........................	19 Sept. 1824

(928)   **ELEAZER FOLGER.**

Son of Peter Folger (905) and Mary Morrill. Born in Nantucket in 1648. Married Sarah Gardner (934) in 1671. Died
in Nantucket about 1716.

CHILDREN.

	Date of Birth.		Date of Birth.
Eleazer, Jr. (m. Beth.Gardner)	1672	Nathan (m. Sarah Church) ..	1673
Peter ....(935)	about 1674	Mary (m. John Arthur)	1684
Sarah (m. Anthony Oder).. .	1676		

(929)   **MARY BARNARD.**

Daughter of Tristram Barnard (939) and Margaret Folger
(940). Born in Stokes Co., N. C., 14 March, 1782. Married
William Macy (927) in Stokes Co., N. C., 1799. Died in Union
Co., Ind., 26 August, 1850.

CHILDREN—See (927).

(930)   **DR. OBED MACY.**

Son of William Macy (927) and Mary Barnard (929). Born
in New Garden, N. C., 14 December, 1801. Married Lucinda
Polk (932) in Bunceville, Ind., 17 October, 1824.

Dr. Obed Macy and family moved to California, where those

still living are now residing.   On the first day of March, 1850, he, with his entire family, consisting of his wife and eight children, left the town of Washington, Davis Co., Ind., with ox-teams for California.   They crossed the State of Illinois, and camped at the town of Kansas in the latter part of March, where his daughter Urania and her husband, D. W. Cheesman (951), joined the party 7 April, 1850.   On 15 May the party left Kansas for California, being in the midst of the great emigration of that year.   On 14 June, Charles was seized with cholera, died, and was buried at Fort Kearney the same day.   On 16 August they arrived at Salt Lake City, having lost twenty-one days out of the first fifty traveling days, by cholera in the train.   They did not dare attempt to cross the Sierras on the northern route, by way of the Humboldt Desert, but re-outfitted at Salt Lake for the southern or Fremont route, and left that place 8 October, 1850; suffered innumerable hardships and privations *en route* by the lack of water and feed for the teams, which nearly all perished thereby.   Arrived in San Francisco 7 February, 1851.   Died in Los Angeles, Cal., 9 July, 1857.

CHILDREN.

	Date of Birth.		Date of Birth.
Amanda (d. 5 Dec. 1826).....	2 Aug. 1825	William.........	4 Sept. 1841
Urania ....(933)	5 Apr. 1828	Obed (m. Mary Sullivan)	23 Nov. 1843
Oscar (m. Margaret Bell)....	7 July 1829	Lucinda (m. Samuel C. Foy).	2 Dec. 1844
Nancy (m. A. L. Woodruff)..	13 Oct. 1832	Mary Jane (m. T. Evans)....	12 July 1849
Louisa (m. John M. Foy)	13 Dec. 1834	Alice (d. 5 Mar. 1854)	2 Oct. 1852
Charles P. (d. 14 June 1850) ..	3 Apr. 1837	Christiana (d. 9 Jan. 1856)....	13 Nov. 1855
Margaret (d. 1845)	17 Sept. 1839		

(931)   **NATHANIEL BARNARD.**

Son of Thomas Barnard and Eleanor   .   Born about 1650.   Married Mary Barnard, a daughter of his uncle, Robert Barnard, and Joanna Harvey.

CHILDREN.

	Date of Birth.		Date of Birth.
Stephen (m. Hep. Hopcott)..	16 Feb. 1674	John (m. Sarah Macy)	
Nathaniel (m. Dor. Manning)		Benjamin (m. Judith Gardner)	
Eleanor (m. Ebenezer Coffin)		Ebenezer (m. Mary Hussey) .	
Mary (m. John Folger).......		Abigail (m. Abram Chase) ...	
Timothy		Sarah (m. —— Currier)